Simply Southern Cakes: 60 Super Simple & #Delish Southern Cake Recipes

RHONDA BELLE

DEDICATION

To Foodies Everywhere...Enjoy & Be Well!

Table of Contents

LET THEM EAT CAKE!..8
   1ST CHRISTMAS CAKE...9
   7 - UP CAKE..9
   ALMOND POUND CAKE...10
   ANGEL FOOD CAKE...10
   APPLESAUCE CAKE...11
   AUNT FRANKIE'S FRUIT CAKE...11
   BANANA CAKE..12
   BLACK MAGIC CAKE...12
   BLACK WALNUT CAKE..13
   BLACKBERRY CHEESECAKE...13
   BLACKBERRY UPSIDE DOWN CAKE......................................14
   BROWN SUGAR PECAN CAKE...15
   BUTTERMILK POUND CAKE..15
   CARAMEL CAKE..16
   CARROT CAKE..16
   CHOCOLATE CHIP CAKE...17
   CHOCOLATE GOURD CAKE...17
   CHOCOLATE PUDDING CAKE...18
   COOL COLA CAKE...18
   DARLING DATE CAKE...19
   DEVIL'S FOOD CAKE...19
   DOWN IN THE DELTA DIRT CAKE...20
   EASY CINNAMON COFFEECAKE...20
   FRESH APPLE CAKE..20
   FRESH ORANGE CHIFFON CAKE..21
   FRUIT CAKE...21
   GERMAN CHOCOLATE CAKE...22
   GOLDEN ANGEL FOOD...23
   GRANDMA'S POUND CAKE...23
   GRILLED POUND CAKE...23
   HOMEMADE CHOCOLATE CAKE...24
   HONEY - OATMEAL CAKE..24
   LEMON MERINGUE CAKE..25
   MACADAMIA MANIA CHEESECAKE.....................................26
   MAPLE NUT CAKE...26
   MAYONNAISE CHOCOLATE CAKE.......................................27
   MOCHA CAKE...27

MOIST PINEAPPLE CAKE 28

NANA'S COCONUT CAKE 28

PEACH CUSTARD CAKE 29

PEACH UPSIDE-DOWN CAKE 29

PEANUT BUTTER CAKE 30

PEAR CAKE 30

PINEAPPLE RAISIN CAKE 31

PINK LADY CAKE 31

PRALINE POUND CAKE 32

PRETTY AS A PEACH CAKE 32

PUMPKIN CAKE 33

RED VELVET CAKE 33

ROYALTY CAKE 34

RUM CAKE 34

SHERRY PRUNE CAKE 35

SOUR CREAM CHOCOLATE CAKE 35

SPICED CRANBERRY CAKE 36

STRAWBERRY SHORTCAKE 36

SUMMER ICE CREAM CAKE 37

SWEETTOOTH CAKE (DIABETIC) 37

TOFFEE CARAMEL "POKE" CAKE 38

TOMATO SOUP CAKE 38

VANILLA BUTTERNUT CAKE 39

ACKNOWLEDGEMENTS

To the love of my life, Johnny.
You are Mommy's greatest inspiration.

To my Mom & Dad (Sunset February 2016)
Love you both...always!

LET THEM EAT CAKE!

Cake is a universal, favorite dessert. Be it a birthday, June wedding or a sweet and simple ending to a fabulous southern dinner, cake just makes everything more special. In Southern tradition, the elegance and presentation of a cake at a special (or everyday) affair, said much about the host or hostess. These recipes offer that same homemade, down-home deliciousness and reflect the spirit of southern hospitality.

Here are some great tips to use along with the 60 Super #Delish recipes in this eBook for moist, decadent cakes that will please any crowd.

- Aim for large eggs (3 whole eggs = 2/3 cup; 3 egg whites = ½ cup). Egg whites produce a softer cake than yolks or whole eggs.
- To enhance the flavor of your cake, add 1 teaspoon of your favorite flavor extract per mix (such as: vanilla, almond, lemon, orange, coconut, butter, peppermint, maple or rum) before mixing ingredients.
- For more even sides, a flatter top and to prevent sticking, do not use cooking spray, oils, margarine or butter to prepare pans. Generously grease the bottom and side of your cake pan with solid shortening and then sprinkle with flour to coat. Tap pan to remove excess flour.
- If you are improvising a recipe by adding ingredients such as sour cream, pudding, sweet liqueurs, etc. be sure to adjust your baking time as well.
- If your mixer has a whisk attachment, use the whisk attachment instead of the paddle, for lighter results.
- Unless otherwise specified, cool cakes in pans 15 to 25 minutes before removing. If necessary, loosen cakes by carefully running a knife around side of pans before removing.
- Many people don't realize it, but cake layers can be baked up to 3 weeks in advance. Bake, let the cakes cool completely and then wrap in foil and freeze. Always thaw completely before frosting.

1ST CHRISTMAS CAKE

¼ cup chopped dried apricots
¼ cup dried currants
¼ cup light brown sugar, packed
¼ cup sliced almonds, finely chopped
¼ teaspoon ground nutmeg
¼ teaspoon salt
½ cup dark raisins
½ cup golden raisins
½ cup sugar
½ teaspoon cinnamon
1 tablespoon freshly grated lemon rind
1 teaspoon baking powder
1½ cups all-purpose flour
2 teaspoons vanilla extract
3 large eggs
1 stick salted butter, softened
Nonstick cooking spray

Preheat the oven to 350 °F. Spray an 8-inch spring form pan with nonstick spray.
Line the bottom and sides with wax paper. Combine the flour, baking powder, nutmeg, cinnamon, and salt in a small bowl. In a separate bowl, beat the butter and sugars together until thoroughly mixed. Add the eggs one at a time, beating well after each addition. Add the vanilla and lemon rind. Stir in the flour mixture and the rest of the ingredients. Bake until a cake tester comes out clean, about one hour. Cool in the pan, then remove and set on a plate to frost. Enjoy!

7 - UP CAKE

½ cup shortening
1 (10 ounces) bottle of 7-Up
1 ½ teaspoon lemon flavoring
1 teaspoon vanilla flavoring
2 sticks butter
3 ½ cup plain flour
3 cups sugar
5 eggs

Preheat oven to 325 degrees. Cream butter and shortening. Mix together sugar and eggs, then flour and 7-Up and then flavoring. Cook in the middle of oven for 1 ½ hours. Remove, cool and frost. Enjoy!

ALMOND POUND CAKE

½ cup butter
½ cup Crisco
2 cups flour, sifted
2 cups sugar
2 teaspoon almond extract
6 eggs
Thinly sliced almonds
GLAZE:
¼ cups water
1 cups sugar
2 tablespoon almond extract

To make the cake: Preheat oven to 325 degrees. Generously grease a large tube shaped pan. Press almonds onto sides and bottom and set aside. Using a hand mixer, cream together butter, Crisco and sugar. Add eggs, one at a time, beating after each addition. Gradually add flour and almond extract. Beat at high speed until well mixed and fluffy. Pour into pan. Bake for 1 hour. *To make the glaze*: Boil sugar and water for 1 minute. Remove from heat. Add almond extract. Pour over lukewarm cake. Leave cake in pan until it has cooled completely. Enjoy!

ANGEL FOOD CAKE

¼ teaspoon salt
½ teaspoon almond extract
½ teaspoon vanilla extract
1 ¼ cups cake flour
1 ½ cups egg whites
1 ¾ cups white sugar
1 teaspoon cream of tartar

Preheat oven to 325 degrees. Beat egg whites until they form stiff peaks, and then add cream of tartar, vanilla extract, and almond extract. In another bowl, sift together flour, sugar, and salt about five times. Gently combine the egg whites with the dry ingredients, and then pour into an ungreased 10 inch tube pan. Bake for about one hour, or until cake is golden brown. Invert cake, and allow it to cool in the pan. When thoroughly cooled, remove from pan and enjoy!

APPLESAUCE CAKE

1 box of raisins
1 cup of black walnuts
1 cup of Crisco
1 cup of pecans
1 cup of strawberry preserves
1 teaspoon of cinnamon
1 teaspoon of cloves
1 teaspoon of nutmeg
2 ½ cup of applesauce
2 cups of sugar
2 eggs
2 teaspoons of baking soda mixed in with the applesauce
2 teaspoons of salt
2 teaspoons of vanilla
4 ½ cups of plain flour

Preheat oven to 300 degrees. Cream the shortening and sugar. Add eggs, strawberry preserves, and applesauce. Mix in the flour and spices. Add the raisins and nuts last and mix all together. Bake for 2 hours. Wrap in aluminum foil (for maximum moistness) until ready to serve. #Delish!

AUNT FRANKIE'S FRUIT CAKE

½ cup orange juice or apricot juice
½ lb. candied cherries, green & red
1 cup Brazil nuts (whole)
1 cup flour
1 cup sugar
1 cup sugar
1 lb. whole dates
1 tablespoon brandy flavoring
1 teaspoon baking powder (rounded)
1 teaspoon vanilla
2 cups English walnut meats
4 egg whites, stiffly beaten
4 egg yolks, beaten

GLAZE:
½ cup sugar
1 cup fruit juice
2 tablespoons corn syrup
2 tablespoons cornstarch (corn flour)

To make cake: Sift together sugar, baking powder and flour. Add whole dates, cherries, walnut meats and Brazil nuts. Add 4 egg yolks, 1 cup sugar, brandy flavoring, orange juice or apricot juice, and vanilla. Mix well. Fold in 4 stiffly beaten egg whites. Pour into tube pan, greased and floured. Bake in 250 degree oven for 1 ½ hours. Cool. Soak a cheesecloth in brandy. Wrap cake in cheesecloth, then in foil. *To make glaze:* Bring the sugar and ½ cup juice to a boil. Dissolve the cornstarch in the remaining juice. Add to the boiling juice and cook till thick. Stir in the corn syrup. Bring back to a boil and remove from heat. Cool and drizzle over cake. Decorate with candied cherries (optional). Enjoy!

BANANA CAKE
¼ teaspoon salt
¾ cup potato starch
1 cup egg substitute
1 tablespoon lemon juice
1 teaspoon lemon zest
1 teaspoon orange zest
2/3 cup sugar
3 very ripe bananas, mashed
6 egg whites
Nonstick cooking spray
Preheat oven to 350 degrees. Spray a tube pan or 10 inch spring form pan with non-stick cooking spray. Beat egg substitute, sugar, and lemon juice thoroughly for about 5 minutes. Stir in mashed bananas, salt, lemon and orange zest. Sift in potato starch. Beat for another minute. In a separate bowl, beat the egg whites until they form soft peaks. Stir ¼ of the egg whites into the batter first, stirring constantly. Gently fold the rest of the egg whites into the batter. Pour the mixture into the prepared pan. Bake for 30-40 minutes, or until a toothpick comes out clean and the top is nicely browned. Allow the cake to cook completely on a rack. #Delish!

BLACK MAGIC CAKE
½ cup vegetable oil
¾ cup cocoa
1 cup black coffee
1 cup sour milk
1 teaspoon baking powder
1 teaspoon salt
1 teaspoon vanilla
2 cups flour
2 cups sugar
2 eggs
2 teaspoon baking soda

Preheat oven to 350 degrees. Mix all ingredients together thoroughly into a thin batter. Bake for 35 to 40 minutes. Remove from oven, allow to cook and frost per your preference. Enjoy!

BLACK WALNUT CAKE
½ teaspoon of baking powder
½ teaspoon of baking soda
½ teaspoon of salt
1 cup buttermilk
1 cup cooking oil
1 cup of chopped black walnuts
1 cup of flaked coconut
2 cups of sugar
2 teaspoons of coconut extract
3 cups of flour
4 eggs, beaten
COCONUT SYRUP:
1 cup sugar
2 tablespoons butter
½ cup milk
1 teaspoon of coconut extract

To make cake: Preheat the oven to 325 degrees. Combine the sugar, oil and eggs and beat well. In another bowl, combine all dry ingredients and add to sugar mixture alternately with the buttermilk. Next, stir in nuts and coconut extract. Bake for 1 hour and 5 minutes in a greased and floured tube pan. Pour hot coconut syrup over hot cake. *To make syrup*: Mix ingredients and boil for five minutes. Enjoy!

BLACKBERRY CHEESECAKE
¼ cup butter
¼ cup sugar
½ package of blackberries, thawed
½ pint sour cream
1 ¼ cup graham cracker crumbs
1 cup sugar
1 jar blackberry jam
1 package cream cheese
1 tablespoon cinnamon
1 teaspoon vanilla
3 tablespoons sugar
4 eggs

To make cake: Preheat oven to 300 degrees. Combine crumbs, sugar, cinnamon, and butter and press into the bottom of a spring form pan. Whip cream cheese. Add eggs, one at a time, stirring after each addition. Gradually add sugar and continue to whip mixture. Pour into crust. Bake for 45 minutes and remove from oven. *To make topping*: Whip sour cream, sugar and vanilla together and pour on top of baked cake. Bake for 10 more minutes. Remove, cool and chill in the refrigerator for 4-6 hours. When ready to serve, heat jam and blackberries. Pour hot over the cake slices. #Delish!

BLACKBERRY UPSIDE DOWN CAKE
¼ cup milk
½ cup butter, softened
½ teaspoon salt
1 ½ cups all-purpose flour
1 cup white sugar
1 teaspoon vanilla extract
2 eggs
2 teaspoons baking powder
TOPPING:
¼ cup brown sugar
¾ cup white sugar
2 cups fresh blackberries
2 tablespoons butter
Preheat oven to 350 degrees. *To make topping*: Melt brown sugar and 2 tablespoons butter together in a saucepan over medium heat. Add blackberries to brown sugar mixture; cook and stir until mixture bubbles. Stir ¾ cup white sugar into berries, crushing berries slightly with a fork, and continue cooking until berries are hot and mushy, about 5 minutes more. Remove from heat and pour into a 9-inch cake pan. *To make cake*: Beat 1 cup sugar and ½ cup butter together in a bowl with an electric mixer until light and fluffy; beat in eggs. Whisk flour, baking powder, and salt together in a bowl. Alternately stir flour and milk into butter mixture, beginning and ending with the flour mixture. Mix vanilla into batter. Pour batter over blackberry mixture in the pan. Bake until cooked through, about 35 to 40 minutes. Let cake cool in the pan until warm, but not completely cooled, about 30 minutes. Run a knife along the inside edge of the pan to separate cake from the sides, place a cake plate over the top of the pan, and flip. Lift the pan slowly to release the cake from the pan (revealing beautiful berry topping). Enjoy!

BROWN SUGAR PECAN CAKE

½ teaspoon baking soda
1 ¼ cups brown sugar, packed
1 cup butter, softened
1 cup nonfat plain yogurt
1 teaspoon baking powder
1 teaspoon vanilla
2 cups all-purpose flour
2 eggs

TOPPING:

¼ cup brown sugar, packed
½ teaspoon ground allspice
½ teaspoon ground nutmeg
1 cup pecans, coarsely chopped

To make cake: Heat oven to 350 degrees. Grease tube pan. Stir together flour, baking powder, baking soda; set aside. With electric mixer, beat butter and brown sugar until fluffy. In another small bowl, beat in eggs, yogurt and vanilla. Gradually beat flour mixture into the batter until well blended. *To make topping:* Combine the pecans, brown sugar, nutmeg, and allspice and set aside. Sprinkle ¼ of the topping into the prepared pan first. Spoon on one-third of the batter. Continue layering. Bake in a 350 degree oven for 50 to 60 minutes or until toothpick inserted in center comes out clean. Cool 15 minutes in pan; remove from pan to a rack; serve warm. Enjoy!

BUTTERMILK POUND CAKE

¼ teaspoon of baking soda
½ teaspoon of salt
½ teaspoon of vanilla
½ teaspoon so butter flavoring
1 cup of buttermilk
1 teaspoon of almond extract
1 teaspoon of lemon extract
2 sticks of butter
3 cups of sugar
3 cups sifted flour
6 eggs, separated

Preheat oven to 350 degrees. Mix butter and sugar at medium speed. Add the egg yolks one at a time, mixing after adding each addition. Add the flavorings. Sift the flour, salt and baking soda together. Add the dry ingredients to the butter and egg mixture, alternating with buttermilk in the beginning and ending with dry ingredients. Beat egg whites until stiff but not dry and fold into the mixture. Pour into a greased and floured 10- inch tube pan. Bake for 1 hour and 15 min. Allow to cool for 15 minutes before removing from pan. Enjoy!

CARAMEL CAKE
½ teaspoon salt
1 cup milk
1½ teaspoons artificial vanilla flavoring
2 cans sweetened condensed milk
2 cups sugar
2 sticks butter, softened
2½ teaspoons baking soda
3 cups flour (cake flour can be substituted)
4 eggs

In a large pot, **completely cover** 2 cans of unopened canned milk in water. This is important. Boil on medium heat for 3½ hours, making sure that cans are turned over every 30 minutes (different sides and then top & bottom). Use a timer for this process and add more water as needed. When done, preheat oven to 350 degrees. In a large mixing bowl, mix butter and sugar with a spoon until smooth. Put all dry ingredients in a separate bowl and mix. Using a hand mixer, add eggs, 1 at a time. Pour in parts of the dry mixture and then milk, alternating each. Add flavor. Bake in 2 or 3 round or square pans as you see fit. Bake for 25 minutes. Insert toothpicks to check for doneness. Let cool on wire racks before applying your desired frosting. At the same time the cans should have completed their boiling, pour off water and let cool in sink for 15 minutes. Open with a can opener and stir to the bottom. It can be put on each layer of the cake after it has cooled about 5 more minutes. #Delish!

CARROT CAKE
1 cup pecans, cut sm.
1 cup vegetable oil
2 cups flour
2 cups sugar
2 teaspoon baking powder
2 teaspoons baking soda
2 teaspoons cinnamon
4 cups grated carrots
4 eggs
ICING:
½ stick margarine, softened
1 lb. box powdered sugar
2 teaspoons vanilla extract
8 ounces cream cheese, softened

To make cake: Stir all dry ingredients (except pecans and carrots) together and then add eggs and oil. Mix until just blended and then add carrots and pecans. Bake at 375 to 400 degrees for 35 to 40 minutes or until done. *To make icing*: Mix cream cheese and margarine until smooth, add sugar and vanilla and blend. Ice when cake is cool. Enjoy!

CHOCOLATE CHIP CAKE
½ tablespoon vanilla
½ teaspoon salt
½ teaspoon soda
¾ cups water
1 ¼ cups flour
1 cup sugar
1 egg
1/3 cups oil
2 ounces semi-sweet chocolate bars (2 bars melted)
Mix all ingredients until well blended. Sprinkle ½ package miniature chocolate chips on top. Add nuts, if desired. Bake in 9-inch pan at 350 degrees for 30 minutes. Enjoy!

CHOCOLATE GOURD CAKE
½ cup chopped dates
½ teaspoon almond extract
½ teaspoon cinnamon
1 ¼ teaspoon baking powder
1 ¼ teaspoon baking soda
1 ½ cup oil
1 ½ teaspoon vanilla
1 cup chopped nuts
1 teaspoon salt
3 cups coarsely grated zucchini (or gourd of choice)
3 cups flour
3 cups sugar
3 ounces melted & cooled chocolate
4 eggs
Sift together flour, baking powder, soda, salt and cinnamon. Set aside. Beat eggs in large bowl until frothy. Gradually beat in sugar and oil. Add chocolate, vanilla and almond extract. Fold in dry ingredients. Squeeze excess moisture from zucchini. Fold zucchini, nuts and dates into batter. Pour into greased and floured 10 inch tube pan. Bake at 350 degrees for 1 hour and 15 minutes to 1 hour and 25 minutes. Test with a toothpick. Let stand inverted on wire rack 20 minutes. Remove pan. Cool, cook completely on rack. #Delish!

CHOCOLATE PUDDING CAKE

1 cup chopped nuts
1 cup flour
1 cup Cool Whip
1 cup powdered sugar
1 small box chocolate instant pudding
1 small box vanilla instant pudding
1 stick oleo
2 cups milk
8 ounces cream cheese

Preheat oven to 350 degrees. Combine oleo, flour and nuts. Press into 9 x 13 inch pan and bake for 20 minutes. Cool. Slice cake and cut a well into both layers. Fill with a creamy blend of cream cheese, powdered sugar and Cool Whip. Stack layers to form a full size cake. Next, mix both pudding packages mixed with 2 cups milk until blended. Top with pudding followed by remaining Cool Whip. #Delish!

COOL COLA CAKE

½ cup butter
½ cup butter or margarine
½ cup buttermilk
½ cup vegetable oil
1 box (16-ounces) of confectioner's sugar
1 ½ cups small marshmallows
1 cup chopped pecans
1 cup Coca-Cola
1 teaspoon baking soda
1 teaspoon vanilla extract
1 teaspoon vanilla extract
2 cups all-purpose flour
2 cups sugar
2 eggs
3 tablespoons cocoa
3 tablespoons cocoa
6 tablespoons Coca-Cola

To make cake: Preheat oven to 350 degrees. In a bowl, sift the sugar and flour. Add marshmallows. In a saucepan, mix the butter, oil, cocoa and Coca-Cola. Bring to a boil and pour over dry ingredients; blend well. Dissolve baking soda in buttermilk just before adding to batter along with eggs and vanilla extract, mixing well. Pour into a well-greased 9- by-13-inch pan and bake 35 to 45 minutes. Remove from oven and frost immediately. *To make frosting*: Combine ½ cup butter, 3 tablespoons cocoa and 6 tablespoons of Coca-Cola in a saucepan. Bring to a boil and pour over confectioner's sugar, blending well.

Add vanilla extract and pecans. Spread over hot cake. When cool, cut into squares and serve. Enjoy!

DARLING DATE CAKE
½ cups nuts, chopped
½ pkg. chocolate chips
½ teaspoon salt
1 ¾ cups all-purpose flour, sifted
1 cup boiling water
1 cup dates, chopped
1 cup shortening
1 cup sugar
1 tablespoon cocoa
1 teaspoon soda
1 teaspoon vanilla
2 eggs, well beaten
Preheat oven to 325 degrees. Combine dates, boiling water and soda. Cool. Cream shortening and sugar. Add eggs. Add date mixture. Sift flour, salt, cocoa, mix; add vanilla. Pour into greased cake pan. Top with chocolate chips and nuts. Bake 40 minutes. This dish makes its own glaze! Can be topped with ice cream or whipped cream. #Delish!

DEVIL'S FOOD CAKE
2 (1-ounce) squares of unsweetened chocolate, melted
¾ teaspoon salt
1 ½ cup sugar
1 cups milk
1 tablespoon hot water
1 teaspoon baking soda
1 teaspoon vanilla
2 cups cake flour
2 eggs
2/3 cup shortening
Sift dry ingredients together, put aside. Cream shortening and sugar together and add eggs. Add dry ingredients alternately with milk to creamed mixture. Add vanilla and melted chocolate and water. Bake for 30 minutes at 350 degrees. Cool and frost with frosting per your unique taste. Enjoy!

DOWN IN THE DELTA DIRT CAKE

1 (8 ounces) cream cheese
1 cup confectioners' sugar
1 large tub Cool Whip
1 pkg. Oreo cookies
1 teaspoon vanilla
2 small boxes vanilla pudding & pie filling
3 cups milk

Crumble ½ package of cookies and cover bottom of 9 x 13 inch pan. Mix milk, vanilla, sugar and cream cheese until creamy. Add pudding and mix until creamy. Pour mixture over cookies in pan. Then add the other ½ package of cookies on pudding. Then top with Cool Whip. #Delish!

EASY CINNAMON COFFEECAKE

2 tablespoons butter or margarine
1 cup packaged biscuit mix
1/3 cup evaporated milk, undiluted
1 tablespoon cinnamon-sugar mixed (half and half)

To make coffeecake: Cut butter into tiny pieces over biscuit mix in medium bowl. Toss lightly with fork until butter is coated. Make a well in center. Pour in milk and cinnamon-sugar, stirring with fork just until mixture is moistened. Turn dough into a lightly greased and floured cast iron skillet. With floured hands, pat down evenly into the skillet. Cook, covered, over very low heat, for 12 to 15 minutes, or until a cake tester or wooden pick inserted in center comes out clean. *To make topping*: Spread the coffeecake with 2 teaspoon butter or margarine. Then sprinkle 1 teaspoon prepared cinnamon-sugar over all of it. Cut into quarters, and serve warm. #Delish!

FRESH APPLE CAKE

½ cup coconut
½ teaspoon vanilla
1 ½ cup sugar
1 ½ teaspoon cinnamon
1 cup oil
1 teaspoon baking powder
1 teaspoon baking soda
1 teaspoon salt
2 ½ cup flour
2 eggs
4 cups apple, finely chopped

Preheat oven to 350 degrees. Beat together oil, sugar, eggs and vanilla. Add apples, and set aside. Sift together flour, salt, baking soda, powder and cinnamon. Add dry ingredients to apple mixture, blending well. Add coconut.

Spread into a greased and floured 9 x 13 inch pan (or two 8 x 8 inch pans). Bake for 35 to 40 minutes. Cool in pan. Serve warm. Enjoy!

FRESH ORANGE CHIFFON CAKE
1 ½ cups sugar
1 teaspoon salt
2 ¼ cups sifted flour
3 teaspoon double-action baking powder
Measure these and sift together into mixing bowl. Make a "well" and add in order:
½ cup vegetable oil
5 unbeaten egg yolks
Grated rind of 2 oranges (about 2 tablespoons)
Juice of 2 oranges and water to make ¾ cups of juice
Beat with spoon until nice and smooth. Next, in a separate mixing bowl, combine:
1 cups egg whites (7 to 8)
½ teaspoon cream of tartar
Whip until whites form extremely stiff peaks. Pour egg yolk mixture gradually over whipped egg whites - gently folding with rubber scraper just until blended. DO NOT STIR! Pour at once into ungreased tube pan. Bake in 325 degree oven for 65 minutes. Immediately turn pan upside down. A great trick here is to place the upside-down pan over the neck of a glass bottle. Let cake hang until it grows cold. Loosen sides and tube with spatula and turn out completely on a plate.
ICING:
1 ½ (3 ounces each) pkgs. cream cheese
2 ¼ cups sifted confectioner's sugar
Grated rind of 2 oranges (1 ½ tablespoon)
Cream the cream cheese until light and fluffy. Gradually add sugar and beat well. Stir in orange rind. If too thick, add a few drops orange juice. Ice sides and top of cake. Enjoy!

FRUIT CAKE
½ cup butter
½ teaspoon milk
½ teaspoon soda
1 quart fresh blueberries (or berries of choice)
1 teaspoon cream of tartar
2 cups sugar
2 eggs, beaten
3 ¼ cups flour

Mix butter and cream sugar by hand. Add eggs and blend well. Add dry ingredients and alternate with milk. Cream until smooth. Add fresh fruit and blend again. Pour into a buttered cake pan. Sprinkle with cinnamon and sugar. Bake for 40 minutes to one hour at 350 degrees. Remove from oven, brush with butter and cool for 15 minutes. Enjoy!

GERMAN CHOCOLATE CAKE

4 ounces chopped or grated organic chocolate
½ cup boiling water
1 cup raw or organic butter, softened
2 cups maple sugar
4 eggs, yolks separated from whites
1-teaspoon vanilla
2 ½ cups wheat flour
1 teaspoon baking soda
½ teaspoon sea salt
1 cup + 3 tablespoons buttermilk

FROSTING (DOUBLE THIS RECIPE TO FROST SIDES OF CAKE)

1 cup light cream
1 cup sugar or sugar substitute
3 egg yolks, beaten
½ cup butter
1 teaspoon vanilla
1 1/3 cups flaked organic coconut
1 cup crispy pecans, toasted and chopped

To make cake: Preheat your oven to 350 degrees. Butter and flour 3 round cake pans. Line each with wax paper or natural parchment. Place chopped or grated chocolate in a small glass or ceramic bowl. Add boiling water and stir until melted. Set aside to cool. In a large bowl, mix butter with sugar until fluffy. Slowly add egg yolks and blend well. Add melted chocolate and vanilla and blend well. In a separate bowl, mix flour, baking soda and salt together. Alternate adding the flour mixture and buttermilk to your batter, beginning and ending with flour. Blend until batter is smooth. In another bowl beat egg whites until stiff peaks form (about 5 minutes). Fold your egg whites slowly into your cake batter. Don't stir or beat them in. Divide your batter between the two prepared cake pans. Bake for 30-40 minutes or until a toothpick inserted in the middle comes out clean. Cool layers for 15 minutes before removing to cooling rack. Slowly remove the wax paper from each inverted layer. *To make frosting*: In a heavy saucepan on medium heat, combine cream, sugar, egg yolks, butter and vanilla. Stir until melted and continue stirring for 12 minutes. Stir in the coconut and toasted pecans. Remove frosting from heat and let cool until firm and easy to spread. Frost a layer and place another on top. Frost top of cake (and sides if frosting recipe has been doubled). #Delish!

GOLDEN ANGEL FOOD
¼ teaspoon salt
½ cup cold water
½ teaspoon baking powder
¾ teaspoon cream of tartar
1 ½ cups cake flour
1 ½ cups sugar
1 teaspoon vanilla
5 eggs

Preheat oven to 350 degrees. Beat egg whites until bubbly. Add cream of tartar and beat until stiff. Set aside while you beat the egg yolks with cold water until fluffy. Add sugar and continue beating until mixture is very light and creamy. (More beating makes a bigger, fluffier cake!) Sift together the dry ingredients and fold carefully into egg yolks. Fold in vanilla. Fold whites into yolk mixture. Bake in angel food cake pan for one hour. Enjoy!

GRANDMA'S POUND CAKE
4 eggs
2 cups sugar
1 cups margarine
3 cups flour
½ teaspoon soda
1 ½ teaspoon baking powder
1 teaspoon vanilla
1 teaspoon lemon extract
1 cups sour milk or buttermilk

Mix all ingredients together until well mixed. Bake at 325 degrees for 60 minutes or until the cake tests done. Enjoy!

GRILLED POUND CAKE
¼ cup unsalted butter, melted
¾ cup dried sour cherries
1 cup boiling water
1/3 cup pecans, toasted and coarsely chopped
1-½ pints vanilla ice cream, softened slightly
16-oz. loaf pound cake, cut into 16 ½-inch slices
4-½ tablespoons semisweet chocolate, coarsely chopped
5 tablespoons brandy

Place cherries in medium bowl. Pour 1 cup boiling water over cherries; let stand until softened, about 10 minutes. Drain and pat dry. Mix cherries and 1 tablespoon brandy in small bowl. Place ice cream in large bowl; mix in cherries, semisweet chocolate and pecans; cover and freeze until firm, about 2 hours.

Prepare barbecue grill with medium heat. Brush both sides of each cake slice with melted butter. Grill slices until lightly toasted, about 30 seconds per side. Place 2 slices of cake on each dessert plate. Place 1 scoop ice cream on top of cake slices. If desired, drizzle 1-½ teaspoon brandy over each serving. #Delish!

HOMEMADE CHOCOLATE CAKE
½ teaspoon of salt
¾ cup of cocoa
1 cup of boiling water
1 cup of milk
1 teaspoon of baking powder
1 teaspoon of baking soda
1 teaspoon of butter
1 teaspoon of vanilla
2 cups of plain flour
2 cups of sugar
2 eggs

Beat the sugar, eggs and butter together until creamy. Add the cocoa to 1 cup of boiling water and mix well. Add cocoa mixture to sugar mixture. Sift flour, soda, baking powder and salt together. Add to the sugar mixture alternating with the milk and vanilla, starting and ending with the flour mixture. Pour into well-greased and floured pans and bake at 350 degrees for 25 to 30 minutes.

FROSTING:
½ cup of milk
1 ½ cup of sugar
1 teaspoon of vanilla
2 (1 ounce) squares of chocolate
2 tablespoons of butter

Melt the chocolate in a pan and remove from heat. Mix in the sugar and milk and bring to a full boil. Cook the chocolate mixture until it reaches the "soft ball stage" (a small amount dropped into a glass of cold water forms a soft ball). Remove the chocolate mixture from the heat and stir in the vanilla and butter. Spread on the cooled cake. #Delish!

HONEY - OATMEAL CAKE
¼ teaspoon ground nutmeg
½ cup butter or margarine, softened
¾ teaspoon salt
1 ¼ cups boiling water
1 ½ cup honey
1 ¾ cups whole wheat flour
1 cup uncooked rolled oats
1 teaspoon baking soda

1 teaspoon ground cinnamon
1 teaspoon vanilla
2 eggs
Pecan halves (optional)

Preheat oven to 350 degrees. Combine water, oats and margarine in a large bowl; stir well. Set aside for 20 minutes. Add honey, eggs and vanilla; stir well. Combine whole wheat flour, soda, salt, cinnamon and nutmeg, gradually add to honey mixture. Pour into a greased and floured cake pan. Bake for 30 to 40 minutes or until toothpick comes out clean. Cool in pan and frost. Garnish with pecan halves and store-bought German chocolate cake frosting. Enjoy!

LEMON MERINGUE CAKE

¼ cup margarine, softened
¼ cup sugar
¼ teaspoon salt
½ cup skim milk
½ cup sugar
1 ¼ cups flour
1 ½ teaspoon baking powder
1 ½ teaspoon grated lemon peel
1 cups sugar
1 teaspoon vanilla
2 cups sliced strawberries
4 egg whites

Mix strawberries and ¼ cup sugar. Cover and refrigerate. Heat oven to 350 degrees. Grease or spray cake pan. Beat flour, 1 cup sugar, margarine, milk, baking powder, lemon peel, vanilla, salt, and 2 egg whites with a hand mixer on low speed for 30 seconds. Beat on high for 2 minutes. Bake 25 to 30 minutes or until cake tester comes out clean. Remove from the oven. Increase oven temp to 400 degrees. Beat 2 egg whites until foamy, adding ½ cup sugar gradually. Beat until stiff and glossy. Spread over cake. Bake an additional 8 to 10 minutes until light brown. Cool completely. Serve with strawberries. #Delish!

MACADAMIA MANIA CHEESECAKE

½ cup macadamia nuts, finely chopped
¾ cup sugar
1 teaspoon vanilla
11 ounces of cream cheese
3 eggs
A dash of salt
One prepared chocolate pie crust

Blend cream cheese, sugar, vanilla and salt. Add eggs one at a time, mixing well after each. Sprinkle nuts over pie crust. Pour filling on top. Set on baking sheet and bake for 35-40 minutes at 325 degrees. #Delish!

MAPLE NUT CAKE

½ cup shortening
¾ cup chopped pecans
1 ¼ cups sugar
1 ¼ teaspoon maple extract
1 cup milk
1 egg
2 ½ cups self-rising flour
2 egg yolks

Place all ingredients (except pecans) in large mixing bowl. Beat at medium speed for 3 to 4 minutes or until well blended. Stir in ¾ cup pecans. Turn into greased cake pan and spread evenly. Bake in at 350 degrees for 35 to 45 minutes or until cake tests done. Remove from oven and cool 5 minutes. Meanwhile, prepare frosting.

MAPLE FROSTING:

¼ cups chopped pecans
¼ cups sugar
¾ teaspoon maple extract
2 egg whites

Beat egg whites until foamy. Gradually beat in sugar, a tablespoonful at a time. Blend in maple extract. Continue beating until soft peaks form. Spread frosting on top of warm cake. Return cake to oven and bake 10 minutes or until frosting is lightly browned. Sprinkle with nuts and enjoy!

MAYONNAISE CHOCOLATE CAKE

1 cup mayo
1 cup sugar
1 cup water
1 egg
1 teaspoon vanilla
2 cups flour
2 teaspoons baking soda
5 tablespoon baking cocoa

Cream sugar and mayonnaise. Add egg and vanilla. Dissolve baking soda in water and add to first mixture. Sift flour and cocoa together and stir into mixture. Pour into a greased baking dish and bake at 350 degrees for 30 minutes. Remove, cool and frost as desired. Enjoy!

MOCHA CAKE

½ cup melted butter
½ cup sugar
1 1/3 cups confectioners' sugar
1 cup sifted flour
1 cup unsalted butter
1 tablespoon rum
1 tablespoon rum
1 teaspoon salt
4 eggs
5 teaspoon instant coffee powder
6 egg yolks

Butter and flour a 9 inch cake pan. Preheat oven to 325 degrees. Put eggs, sugar, salt and rum in a large bowl and beat with the electric mixer until batter is white and thick and spins a very heavy ribbon when falling from the beaters. Next, fold in the flour, followed by the melted butter. DO NOT STIR! Turn into a prepared cake pan and bake 40 minutes on the lowest rack of a 325 degree oven. Invert onto a cake rack, let cool completely and split into 2 layers. *To make the butter cream*: put egg yolks, sugar, and coffee dissolved in rum in a large mixing bowl. Beat until very thick, light in color and spinning a heavy ribbon. Cream in the butter, tablespoon by tablespoon, until it has been completely absorbed. Sprinkle toasted almond slivers all over the cake and dust lightly with confectioners' sugar. Enjoy!

MOIST PINEAPPLE CAKE

1 ½ cup sugar
1 teaspoon vanilla
2 cups flour
2 eggs
2 teaspoon baking soda
20 ounces can crushed pineapple (undrained)
Dash of salt

Combine dry ingredients. Add other ingredients and mix. Pour into a greased and floured 9 inch cake pan and bake about 45 minutes at 325 degrees. Frost with coconut icing.

COCONUT ICING:

½ cup evaporated milk
½ cup nuts
¾ stick margarine (6 tablespoons)
1 cup coconut
1 cup sugar

Melt margarine, add all other icing ingredients and cook icing 2 minutes. Pour over hot cake. #Delish!

NANA'S COCONUT CAKE

½ cup butter or margarine
1 ½ cup all-purpose flour
1 ½ cup boiling water
1 cup granulated sugar
1 cup rolled oats
1 cups light brown sugar
1 teaspoon baking soda
1 teaspoon cinnamon
1 teaspoon vanilla
2 eggs, unbeaten

TOPPING:

¼ lb. butter (or margarine)
1 cup brown sugar
1 cup coconut
1 cup nuts, chopped
1/3 cup milk

To make cake: Preheat oven to 325 degrees. Pour boiling water over oats, stir, and let stand. Mix together butter, sugar, light brown sugar, and eggs. Whip oats and add to butter mixture. Sift together flour, cinnamon, and baking soda and add to the other mixture. Next, add 1 teaspoon vanilla. Pour into greased cake pan(s) and bake for at least 45 minutes or until tested done. *To make topping*: Spread this mixture on cake after removing from oven. Place under broiler. Remove when topping is browned, be careful not to burn. Takes about 5 to 8 minutes in 400 degree broiler. Enjoy!

PEACH CUSTARD CAKE
CRUST:
½ cup soft butter
½ teaspoon salt
1 ½ cup flour
BATTER:
½ cup sugar
½ teaspoon cinnamon
1 cup evaporated milk
1 egg
1 large can sliced peaches, juice divided
Cut butter into flour and salt. Press into 9 inch cake pan. Drain peaches, saving ½ cup of syrup. Arrange slices on top of crust. Sprinkle with mixture of sugar and cinnamon. Bake at 375 degrees for 20 minutes. Remove from oven. Mix remaining syrup, egg and milk. Pour over peaches. Bake for 30 minutes more. Enjoy!

PEACH UPSIDE-DOWN CAKE
¼ teaspoon of salt
½ cup of butter, softened
½ cup of milk
½ teaspoon of baking soda
½ teaspoon of corn starch
1 ½ cup of flour
1 cup plus 2 tablespoons of sugar
1 pound of peaches, peeled and sliced
1 teaspoon of cream of tartar
1 teaspoon of vanilla extract
2 eggs, separated
Preheat the oven to 350 degrees. Spread the peaches into the bottom of a 9-inch cake pan. Sprinkle with 2 tablespoons of the sugar and let sit. Combine the flour, cream of tartar, baking soda, cornstarch and salt in a medium bowl the combine the milk and vanilla in another small bowl and set aside. Cream together the butter and the remaining 1 cup of sugar in a medium bowl. Add the egg yolks one at a time, beating after each addition. Add the milk and flour mixtures in alternating additions, beating continuously. Beat the egg whites until soft peaks form and fold into the batter. Pour the batter evenly over the peaches and bake until a knife inserted in the center comes out clean, or about 1 hour. Let cool slightly and invert onto a serving platter. #Delish!

PEANUT BUTTER CAKE

½ cup brown sugar
½ cup peanut butter
½ teaspoon salt
1 cup brown sugar
1 cup milk
1 teaspoon vanilla
1/3 cups shortening
2 ½ teaspoon baking powder
2 cups flour
2 eggs

Grease two cake pans. Cream shortening. Slowly beat in 1 cup brown sugar and peanut butter. In another bowl, beat together 2 eggs and ½ cup brown sugar. Add this to the first mixture and beat well. Sift together flour, salt and powder. Add dry ingredients alternately to first mixture with 1 cup milk with vanilla. Pour mixture into pans and bake immediately until cakes are firm in the center. Bake at 350 degrees for 30 minutes. Remove and serve warm. #Delish!

PEAR CAKE

½ cup chopped nuts
½ cup margarine
½ teaspoon each nutmeg, ginger, cloves
½ teaspoon salt
1 ½ cup boiling water
1 ½ cup flour
1 cup brown sugar
1 cup rolled oats
1 cup sugar
1 teaspoon baking soda
1 teaspoon cinnamon
1 teaspoon vanilla
2 cups ripe pears, cored & finely chopped
3 eggs

Pour water over oats and allow to sit for ½ hour. Cream butter and sugar; beat in eggs and vanilla. In a large bowl, toss pears with flour, mix in soda, salt, spices and nuts. Fold in oatmeal and egg mixture until thoroughly blended. Pour into greased and floured baking pan. Bake at 350 degrees for 35 to 45 minutes or until wooden pick inserted near center comes out clean. Cool. Serve with whipped topping. Enjoy!

PINEAPPLE RAISIN CAKE

¼ teaspoon salt
½ cup butter or margarine, room temperature
½ cup dark raisins
½ cup 100% pineapple juice
½ cup milk
½ cup sugar
½ teaspoon baking soda
1 ½ cup all-purpose flour
1 cup sugar
1 teaspoon baking powder
2 eggs
4 slices of canned pineapple

Cream butter and sugar until light. Add eggs and beat until fluffy. Stir together flour, baking powder, baking soda and salt. Add to creamed mixture alternately with the milk. Mix until batter is smooth. Stir in the raisins. Cut pineapple into ½ inch pieces and add to the batter. Turn into a well-buttered and floured 6 cup fancy cake or ring mold. Bake at 350 degrees for 45 to 50 minutes or until cake tests done in the center. Meanwhile, heat pineapple juice and sugar to boiling. Remove cake from oven and immediately pour pineapple syrup over. Allow to stand 5 minutes; then turn out onto cooling rack. Cool and serve warm. Enjoy!

PINK LADY CAKE

¼ teaspoon baking soda
¼ teaspoon salt
1 ¼ cups sugar
1 ½ teaspoons baking powder
1 cup butter, softened
1 cup buttermilk
1 teaspoon vanilla extract
1/8 teaspoon pink paste food coloring
2 ½ cups all-purpose flour
3 eggs

In a large bowl, cream the butter, sugar and food coloring until light and fluffy. Add eggs, one at a time, beating well after each addition. Beat in vanilla. Combine the flour, baking powder, baking soda and salt; add to creamed mixture alternately with buttermilk, beating well after each addition. Pour into greased and floured cake pans. Bake at 350° for 23-27 minutes. Cool for 10 minutes before frosting per your choice. Enjoy!

PRALINE POUND CAKE

1 cup butter
2 cups sugar
4 eggs
4 cups flour
1 teaspoon baking soda
1 teaspoon baking powder
4 ounces sour cream
4 ounces cream cheese; softened
1 cup praline liqueur
1 cup pecans; chopped

GLAZE:

¼ cup butter
½ cup brown sugar
¼ cup praline liqueur
1/8 cup water

To make cake: Preheat oven to 350 degrees. Cream butter and sugar. Add eggs and beat 3 minutes. Mix together the flour, baking soda, and baking powder. Next, in another bowl, combine sour cream, cream cheese and liqueur. Alternately add dry ingredients with cheese mixture, beating well. Stir in pecans. Grease and flour a Bundt pan and pour batter. Bake for 60-70 minutes. Remove from oven, cool 15 minutes then glaze. *To make glaze*: Combine the butter, brown sugar, praline liqueur, and water all in a small saucepan; bring to a boil. Stir for 5 minutes. Pour over cake. Enjoy!

PRETTY AS A PEACH CAKE

½ cup chopped nuts
1 ¾ cups sugar
1 cup oil
1 teaspoon cinnamon
1 teaspoon salt
2 cups diced canned peaches
2 cups flour
3 eggs, well beaten
Powdered sugar

Mix all ingredients thoroughly by hand. Pour in greased and floured round cake pan. Bake in 350 degree oven for 40 minutes or until toothpick comes out clean. Sprinkle warm cake with powdered sugar. #Delish!

PUMPKIN CAKE

¼ lb. chop walnuts
1 ½ teaspoon salt
1 cup canned pumpkin
1 cup oil
1 teaspoon cinnamon
1 teaspoon nutmeg
2 cups sugar
2 teaspoon baking soda
2/3 cup water
3 cups flour
4 eggs, well beaten

Combine beaten eggs, nutmeg, cinnamon, sugar, oil and salt. Beat well. Add baking soda, flour, water and pumpkin. Beating again, by hand add walnuts. Place in 2 loaf pans. Bake at 350 degrees for 1 hour. Remove, cool and frost per your desired taste or simply serve plain and warm with coffee. Enjoy!

RED VELVET CAKE

½ cup butter
1 cup buttermilk (or 1 teaspoon vinegar mixed with 1 cup milk)
1 tablespoon cocoa powder
1 teaspoon baking soda stirred into 1 tablespoon vinegar
1 teaspoon vanilla extract
1½ cups sugar
2 cups flour
2 eggs
2 ounces red food coloring

Preheat oven to 350 degrees. Grease two 9" round cake pans, line them with parchment, grease them again and dust them with flour. Cream the butter and sugar. Add the eggs and beat well. Sift the flour and cocoa three times and add them, alternating with the buttermilk, to the butter-sugar mixture. Add food coloring and vanilla. Fold in the baking soda/vinegar combo but do not beat. Pour into cake pans and bake for 25 to 30 minutes, or until a tester comes out clean.

TOPPING:

¼ cup flour
1 cup butter
1 cup milk
1 cup powdered sugar
2 teaspoons vanilla
Blueberries or shredded coconut (optional)

To make the cake: Mix milk and flour in a medium saucepan until blended. Cook slowly until thick like glue, stirring constantly. Cool completely. *To make frosting:* Cream butter and sugar until fluffy, then add to the flour/milk mixture and beat well. Beat in vanilla. The frosting should look like whipped cream when it's ready. Frost the cake layers independently, then stack and frost the sides. Top, if desired, with blueberries, red hots, or shredded coconut. #Delish!

ROYALTY CAKE
¼ cup chopped candied ginger
½ cup shelled pistachios, whole or broken
¾ cup dried apricots, coarsely chopped
¾ cup dried cherries
¾ cup granulated baker's sugar
1 tablespoon lemon juice
1/3 cup chopped candied citrus peel (optional)
10 tablespoons butter, softened
1½ cups all-purpose flour
2 eggs
2/3 cup golden raisins
3 tablespoons orange juice
Parchment paper for easier removal
Zest of one lemon
Zest of one orange
Coat parchment paper and sides of a spring form pan with cooking spray. Beat butter and sugar with an electric mixer until creamy. Beat in eggs. Add flour and mix well. Stir in dried fruits, citrus peel, and ginger. Mix well. Add zest and juices. Stir just to combine. Pour into prepared pan and smooth top. Bake 45 minutes; reduce temperature to 300 degrees and continue baking for an additional 1 hour and 15 to 30 minutes or until golden brown and dry crumbs cling to a pick inserted in center. The top will be slightly cracked. Cool in pan for 15 minutes. Remove sides and cool completely. Wrap well and refrigerate for up to 1 month. If before the holidays, try drizzling periodically with alcohol of choice or fruit juice during the month. Enjoy!

RUM CAKE
½ cup amber colored rum of choice (Bacardi works great)
½ cup cold water
½ cup cooking oil
1 cup chopped pecans or walnuts
1 package vanilla instant pudding mix
1 package yellow cake mix
4 eggs
GLAZE:
¼ cup water

½ cup amber rum
½ cup butter
1 cup sugar

To make cake: Preheat oven to 325 degrees. Sprinkle nuts over bottom of greased 10 inch tube pan or 12 cup Bundt pan. Stir together cake mix, pudding mix, eggs, water, oil and rum. Pour batter over nuts. Bake for 1 hour. Cool 10 minutes in pan. Invert onto serving plate and prick top. *To make glaze*: Melt butter in saucepan. Stir in water and sugar. Let boil for 5 minutes, stirring constantly. Remove from heat and stir in rum. Brush glaze evenly over top and sides of cake. Allow cake to absorb glaze. Repeat until glaze is used up. Enjoy!

SHERRY PRUNE CAKE

½ cup milk
½ cup sherry
1 cup chopped walnuts
1 cup cooked prunes, cooled & chopped
1 cup oil
1 teaspoon each: salt, baking powder, baking soda, nutmeg, cloves, allspice, cinnamon
2 cups flour
2 cups sugar
3 eggs

Combine sherry and milk. Add oil and eggs and mix well. Add the rest of the ingredients and mix well. Bake in a tube or Bundt pan at 325 degrees for 1 to 1 ½ hours or until it tests done. Remove and cool. Enjoy!

SOUR CREAM CHOCOLATE CAKE

¼ cup shortening
½ teaspoon baking powder
¾ cup sour cream
1 ¼ teaspoon salt
1 cup water
1 teaspoon vanilla
2 cups flour
2 cups sugar
2 eggs
4 ounces unsweetened chocolate, melted

FROSTING:
½ cups sour cream
1/3 cups butter
2 teaspoon vanilla
3 cups confectioners' sugar

3 ounces unsweetened chocolate, melted

To make cake: Preheat oven to 350 degrees. Grease and flour cake pan. Measure all cake ingredients into large mixing bowl. Mix for a ½ minute on low speed, scraping bowl constantly. Beat 3 minutes at high speed, scraping bowl occasionally. Pour into pan and bake 40 to 45 minutes. *To make frosting:* Mix butter and chocolate thoroughly. Blend in sugar. Stir in sour cream and vanilla. Beat until smooth. #Delish!

SPICED CRANBERRY CAKE

½ cup canned cranberry sauce
½ cup nuts, chopped
½ cup shortening
½ cup sour cream or buttermilk
½ teaspoon salt
½ teaspoon soda
1 ½ cup flour
1 cup brown sugar
1 teaspoon cinnamon
1 teaspoon nutmeg
2 eggs

Preheat oven to 350 degrees. Cream shortening and brown sugar. Add eggs, sift flour, cinnamon, nutmeg and soda. Combine the creamed mixture with sour cream and cranberry sauce. Best if baked in muffin pans pre-sprayed with nonstick cooking spray for 25 minutes. Remove, cool and enjoy!

STRAWBERRY SHORTCAKE

¼ cup butter
¼ cup solid shortening
¼ cup sugar or honey
½ cup sour cream
½ teaspoon salt
2 cups sifted all-purpose flour
2 cups whipping cream
2 teaspoon orange juice
4 tablespoon sugar
4 tablespoon sugar (optional)
4 teaspoon baking powder
Grated rind from 1 orange

Whipped cream (whip ice cold cream with sugar) until soft peaks form. Combine sliced berries, sugar or honey and orange juice. Let stand at room temperature for 1 hour. Sift all dry ingredients together into a medium bowl. Add orange rind. Add butter and shortening and work them into flour mixture thoroughly. Lightly mix in sour cream with a fork to form a soft dough. Roll

dough out onto lightly floured board, ¾ inch thick. Cut into 4 circles, about .
inches wide (use a 2-pound coffee can as a cutter). Place on ungreased baking
sheet. Bake at 400 degrees about 20 minutes or until golden.   While still
warm, use fork and split cakes in half. Place each on dessert plate. Top with
drained berries and second half of cake. Top with additional berries, ladle
some juice on top. Garnish with whipped cream and a strawberry. #Delish!

SUMMER ICE CREAM CAKE
¾ cup all-purpose flour
1 ¾ quarts vanilla ice cream, softened
1 cup (6 ounces) semisweet chocolate chips
1 cup sugar
1 egg
1 tablespoon shortening
1 teaspoon grated orange peel
1 teaspoon vanilla extract
1/3 cup baking cocoa
3 tablespoons butter, melted
3 tablespoons orange yogurt
4 to 6 ounces semisweet chocolate, chopped
Mixed fresh berries
Line an 8-in. square baking dish with foil and grease the foil; set aside. In a
large bowl, combine the sugar, butter, yogurt, egg, orange peel and vanilla until
blended. Combine flour and cocoa; stir into sugar mixture. Add chocolate
chips. Spread into prepared cake pan. Bake at 325 degrees for 20-25 minutes.
Cool completely on a wire rack. Spread ice cream over cake. Cover and freeze
for 3 hours or until firm. Remove from the freezer 10 minutes before serving.
Optional: In a microwave-safe bowl, melt chocolate and shortening; stir until
smooth. Using foil, lift dessert out of dish; gently peel off foil. Cut into squares.
Garnish with berries and drizzle with chocolate. #Delish!

SWEETTOOTH CAKE (DIABETIC)
¼ teaspoon cinnamon
¼ teaspoon nutmeg
¼ teaspoon salt
1 cup cold water
1 cup dates, chopped
1 cup nuts, chopped
1 cup prunes, chopped
1 cup raisins
1 cups plain flour
1 stick margarine, melted
1 teaspoon baking soda

1 teaspoon vanilla
2 eggs
Preheat oven to 350 degrees. Boil dates and prunes in the one cup of water for 3 minutes; add margarine and raisins and let cool. Mix flour, soda, salt, eggs, nuts, spices and vanilla. Add to fruit mixture. Stir to blend. Pour into baking dish. Bake for 25 to 30 minutes. Remove, cool and enjoy!

TOFFEE CARAMEL "POKE" CAKE
1 pkg. chocolate cake mix
1 jar butterscotch-caramel ice cream topping
1 carton frozen whipped topping, thawed
3 Heath candy bars (1.4 ounces each), chopped
Prepare and bake cake according to package directions, using a greased 13x9-in. baking pan. Cool on a wire rack. Using the handle of a wooden spoon, poke holes in cake. Pour 3/4 cup caramel topping into holes. Spoon remaining caramel over cake. Top with thawed Cool Whip. Sprinkle with candy. Refrigerate for at least 2 hours before serving. #Delish!

TOMATO SOUP CAKE
¼ cup water
½ cups vegetable shortening
½ teaspoon ground cloves
1 ½ teaspoon allspice
1 1/3 cups sugar
1 can tomato soup
1 cup chopped nuts
1 cup raisins
1 teaspoon baking soda
1 teaspoon cinnamon
2 cups flour
2 eggs
4 teaspoon baking powder
Preheat oven to 350 degrees. Sift dry ingredients together. Add shortening and soup. Beat at low speed 2 minutes. Add eggs and water; beat at medium speed 2 minutes. Stir in raisins and nuts. Pour into 10 inch tube pan (greased and floured). Bake for 45 - 50 minutes. Frost with cream cheese frosting when cool. Enjoy!

VANILLA BUTTERNUT CAKE

½ cup Crisco
½ teaspoon salt
1 cup milk
2 sticks margarine
3 cups flour
3 cups sugar
4 teaspoons butternut vanilla flavoring
6 eggs
Nuts of choice

Cream together sugar, margarine and Crisco until very smooth. Add eggs, one at a time, beating until smooth after each. Next add flour with ½ teaspoon salt alternating with 1 cup of milk, ending with flour. Fold in flavoring and nuts by hand. Pour into greased tube pan. Put in cold oven and set temperature at 325 degrees. Bake 1 hour and 45 minutes. *Do not open oven door during baking.* Remove from pan immediately. Frost per personal taste. #Delish!

Thank you for your purchase!
May you enjoy and be well!

ABOUT THE AUTHOR

I am a Tennessee native and a connoisseur of great tastes. My culinary delights are inspired by my Southern roots.

I am from cornbread and cabbage, fried chicken and Kool-Aid soaked lemon slices.

I am from hen houses, persimmon trees and juicy, red tomatoes on the vine.

I am from sunflowers growing wild in summer and homemade ice cream in the winter.

I am from family reunions, blue collar men, happy housewives, and Sunday dinners.

I am from spiritual folks who didn't always get it right, but believed in the power of prayer – and taught it to their kids.

I am from the hottest of hot summers and kids running barefoot and free through thirsty Tennessee grass.

I am from a grandmother who sang gospel that was magic…song drenched air would tumble from her lungs, leap into your spirit and make you feel fantastic things.

I am from hard, heartfelt lessons about living and kitchens full of the perfume of love.

♥♥♥ This book is from my heart to yours. ♥♥♥

For freebies & new book announcements, follow @SoDelishDish on social media!

Scan with your smartphone!

Printed in Great Britain
by Amazon

81979444R00025